MORTON RHUE

Level 2

Retold by Kieran McGovern
Series Editors: Andy Hopkins and Jocelyn Potter

Pearson Education Limited
Edinburgh Gate, Harlow,
Essex CM20 2JE, England
and Associated Companies throughout the world.

ISBN 0 582 41677 9

First published in the USA by Dell Publishing Co., Inc. 1981
First published in Great Britain by Puffin Books 1982
This adaptation first published by Penguin Books 1996
Published by Addison Wesley Longman Limited and Penguin Books Ltd. 1998
New edition first published 1999

5 7 9 10 8 6

Typeset by RefineCatch Limited, Bungay, Suffolk
Set in 11/14pt Monotype Bembo
Printed in Spain by Mateu Cromo, S.A. Pinto (Madrid)

Published by Pearson Education Limited in association with
Penguin Books Ltd., both companies being subsidiaries of Pearson Plc

For a complete list of titles available in the Penguin Readers series please write to your local
Pearson Education office or contact: Penguin Readers Marketing Department,
Pearson Education, Edinburgh Gate, Harlow, Essex, CM20 2JE.

Contents

		page
Introduction		v
Chapter 1	Hitler and the Nazis	1
Chapter 2	Winners Need Discipline!	4
Chapter 3	The Team	9
Chapter 4	Members of the Wave	11
Chapter 5	A Dangerous Experiment	15
Chapter 6	Anger and Fights	20
Chapter 7	At the Football Game	23
Chapter 8	Laurie's Story	24
Chapter 9	A Sad Day for David	27
Chapter 10	The Wave Must End!	31
Chapter 11	The Last Rally	34
Chapter 12	After the Wave	39
Activities		40

Introduction

Mr Ross showed the students a big picture of a wave. 'This is a wave. A wave is something that's always moving. We'll call our team the Wave.'

The Wave started in Mr Ross's history lesson. Now everybody in the school knows about it. Most students love the Wave. Ben Ross loves it too. But Ben's wife, Christy, does not like it. She thinks it is dangerous.

Laurie Saunders is one of Mr Ross's students. She liked the Wave when it started. But now she sees things she does not like. And some students do not want to be in the Wave – what about them?

Can Laurie make the other students see what is happening? The Wave is always moving – can anybody stop it?

The things in *The Wave* really happened in America – in a school in Palo Alto, California. Palo Alto is about fifty kilometres south of San Francisco. It is near the sea and the mountains. The weather is good all year.

In 1969 a history teacher called Ron Jones started the Wave in one of his lessons. He wanted to teach his students about the Nazis in World War II. He wanted them to understand what happened to people in Germany at that time. But something strange happened to his students! Later he said: 'The Wave was the most frightening thing I ever saw in a school. For three years after it, no one talked about it.'

Ron Jones later wrote a short story about the Wave. There was also a one-hour television film. Morton Rhue wrote his book called *The Wave* in 1981.

Chapter 1   Hitler and the Nazis

Ben Ross taught history at Gordon High School. One afternoon he showed a film about Hitler and the Nazis.* At the end of the film, he told his students: 'The Nazis killed more than ten million men, women and children.'

A student near the door turned the lights on. Ben looked round. He saw sad faces all round the room.

'I know many of you are very sad,' Ben told the students, 'But I want you to think about what you saw. Does anybody have any questions?'

Amy Smith put her hand up. 'What was the place in the film called?'

'It was called Auschwitz. The Nazis built Auschwitz to kill people quickly.'

The room was very quiet. Amy put her hand up again. 'Were all the Germans Nazis?' she asked.

'No, most Germans were not Nazis.'

'Did the German people try to stop them?' Amy asked.

'No, most Germans didn't try to stop the Nazis,' Ben told her. 'Perhaps they were afraid of them.'

'But why were they afraid?'

'You must remember that life was very hard in Germany at that time,' said Ben. 'There weren't very many Nazis but they had guns. And after 1945 most Germans said, "We didn't know that they killed all those people. We didn't know about Auschwitz."'

Now Laurie Saunders put her hand up. 'I can't believe that,' she said. 'I think they knew what happened.'

Ben was happy that his students were interested. They were not usually interested in history. 'Only they know what they knew,'

* Adolf Hitler and the Nazis led Germany between 1933 and 1945.

Ben told Laurie. 'And we don't know why most German people did not try to stop the Nazis.'

It was time for lunch. The students left the room quickly. David Collins looked over at Laurie. 'Come on, Laurie,' he said. 'Let's go to lunch. I'm hungry.'

'I'll be down in a few minutes, David,' said Laurie.

David went off to lunch. There were only a few students left in the room now. Laurie looked up at Mr Ross.

'How many people did the Nazis kill?' Laurie asked her teacher.

'They killed more than six million Jews. And about four million others.'

'But why did they kill them? Were all the Nazis bad people?'

Mr Ross put his books in his bag. For about a minute he was quiet. Then he turned to Laurie. 'I don't know, Laurie,' said Mr Ross. 'I can't answer that question.'

◆

A few minutes later, Laurie sat next to David in the school restaurant.

'Look at Robert Billings,' said David. 'Nobody wants to sit with him.'

Robert tried to sit next to two students from Mr Ross's history lesson. The students stood up and went to another table.

'Do you think there's something wrong with him?' Laurie asked.

'I don't know,' said David. 'He's very strange. But perhaps that's because he doesn't have any friends.'

David began eating again. Laurie did not eat any of her lunch. Her face was very sad.

'What's wrong?' David asked.

'That film, David,' Laurie answered. 'I thought it was very sad. Did you think it was sad?'

'Yes, but those things happened a long time ago,' said David. 'You can't change what happened then.'

'But we mustn't forget that it did happen,' Laurie said.

'Look at Robert Billings. Nobody wants to sit with him.'

Amy Smith and Brian Amman came over to their table.

'I want to sit here,' said Amy. 'I was here first!'

'No, I want to sit here,' said Brian. 'I want to talk to David about our football team. We're playing Clarkstown on Saturday.'

'And I want to talk to Laurie about *The Grapevine*.'

David played football for the Gordon High team. Laurie wrote for the school newspaper. It was called *The Grapevine*.

Laurie laughed. 'It's OK, there are two places,' she said.

Brian and Amy sat down.

'Will you win on Saturday?' Laurie asked. 'I'm going to write about the game for next week's *Grapevine*.'

'I don't know,' said David. 'Our players don't have much discipline.'

'That's right,' said Brian. 'And we don't have any good new players.'

◆

Later, Amy Smith and Laurie Saunders sat in the office of *The Grapevine*.

'That was a very sad film,' Amy said. 'What did David think of it?'

'David doesn't think about sad things,' said Laurie. 'All he thinks about is football.'

'What are you and David going to do next year?' Amy asked.

'I don't know,' said Laurie. 'I don't know what we'll do when we finish school. Perhaps we'll go away together. I love David, but I don't know what is going to happen to us. We're very young.'

Chapter 2   Winners Need Discipline!

That afternoon Ben Ross bought some books about the Nazis. They were for his history class. He wanted his students to understand about life in Germany at the time of the Nazis.

4

That afternoon Ben Ross bought some books about the Nazis.

When Christy Ross came home she found her husband at the kitchen table.

'Why are you reading all these books about the Nazis?' Christy asked.

'One of my students asked me a question about them,' said Ben. 'And I don't think they can learn the answer from a book. But I have a plan.'

The next morning Ben went to class early. When the students arrived they saw some words at the front of the room.

'WINNERS NEED DISCIPLINE,' somebody read. 'What does that mean?'

Ben walked over and stood next to David and Brian. 'You two both play football. You know you need discipline to win.'

'We never win,' Eric said, and the class laughed.

'Perhaps that's because you don't have any discipline,' Ben said.

The students were all quiet now. Ben was surprised to see that they were interested. He took his chair and put it at the front of the room.

'Discipline starts with how you sit. I don't want you to sit back in your chairs. You must sit up. Amy, come up here.'

Mr Ross showed Amy how to sit up. Other students began to do the same. Ben walked round the room.

'Look at Robert, everybody,' said Ben. 'He's sitting up. That's very good, Robert.'

Robert looked up at his teacher and smiled.

Ben returned to the front of the room. 'Now I want you all to get up and walk round the room. When I tell you, you must go back to your desks.'

The students stood up and began walking round the room. Ben watched them. Then he said, 'Go back to your places!'

Everybody ran back to their places. 'That wasn't very good!' said Ben. 'Next time I want much more discipline.'

The class got up and went back to their places many times. Each time they did it faster.

'Now there are two more rules,' Ben told the students. 'They're for when you ask or answer a question. The first rule is that you must stand up next to your chairs when you ask or answer a question. The second rule is that you must say 'Mr Ross' before you give your answer.'

Mr Ross walked round the room. He stopped at Brad's desk.

'Brad, who was the leader of the Nazis?'

Brad did not stand up. 'I think it was . . .'

'Wrong, Brad!' said Mr Ross. 'You're forgetting the rules.' Ben looked across the room at Robert. 'Robert, what do we do when we answer a question?'

Robert stood up next to his desk. 'Mr Ross.'

'That's right,' Mr Ross said. 'Thank you, Robert.'

'I don't like this,' said Brad.

'That's because you can't do it,' somebody said. The others laughed.

'Brad,' Mr Ross said, 'who was the leader of the Nazis?'

Brad stood up slowly and stood next to his desk. 'Mr Ross, I think it was Adolf Hitler.'

'You're too slow, Brad,' Mr Ross said. 'I want everybody to give me their answers quickly. Now, Brad, try again.'

Brad jumped up next to his place. 'Mr Ross, it was Hitler.'

Mr Ross smiled. 'That's better,' he said.

After the lesson the students talked together about it.

'That was strange!' said Brian. 'But I thought it was great!'

'I did too,' said Eric.

Amy laughed. 'Anything is better than history,' she said.

'No, don't laugh,' said David. 'This is important. It felt different when we did those things together.'

'Why was it important?' said Brad. 'Ross asked us questions and we answered them.'

'But we were a team!' said David. 'Do you remember what Mr Ross said about discipline? I think he was right. We need that discipline for our football team.'

◆

Late that night Ben talked to his wife about his students.

'Usually they don't do anything I tell them,' he said. 'But they loved the new discipline. I was very surprised.'

'Perhaps they thought it was a game,' said Christy. 'And they all wanted to be the best in the class.'

'I think that's true,' Ben told his wife. 'But the strangest thing was that they wanted me to discipline them. At the end of the lesson they stayed in their places. It was more than a game to them.'

Christy laughed. 'They stayed at the end of the lesson! That's new! Are you going to do the same thing tomorrow?'

'I don't think I will,' said Ben.

'Do you remember what Mr Ross said about discipline? I think he was right.'

Chapter 3   The Team

The next day Ben arrived late for his lesson. When he came into the room his students stood up. Ben was surprised. He looked round the room.

'What are you doing?' he asked.

The students looked at him but nobody spoke.

Ben walked to the back of the room. 'Robert, can you tell me what's happening here?'

Robert jumped up next to his desk. 'Mr Ross, discipline.'

'Yes, discipline,' said Mr Ross. 'But there's something more.' He went back to the front and wrote, 'WE ARE ALL IN THE SAME TEAM' next to 'WINNERS NEED DISCIPLINE'.

Mr Ross turned back to the class. 'Everybody must believe in those words,' he said. 'Now I want us to say them together.'

Round the room students jumped up and said, 'We're all in the same team. Winners need discipline.'

Laurie was the last person to stand up. Now all the students stood next to their desks.

Mr Ross showed the students a big picture of a wave. 'This is a wave. A wave is something that's always moving. We'll call our team the Wave'.

Mr Ross looked round the class. He saw that his students wanted to hear more about the Wave 'This will be our salute,' he said. Ben put his right hand up and moved it up and down. 'Look, my hand is a wave in the sea,' he said. Then he put his hand on his left arm. 'Class, give our salute,' he said.

The students gave the salute. Many did it wrong. 'Do it again,' said Mr Ross. He showed them the salute again. They all did it again and again.

'Good,' said Mr Ross. 'Now everybody can do the Wave salute. This is our salute and our salute only. When you see a Wave

'This is our salute and our salute only. When you see a Wave member, you must salute.'

member, you must salute. Robert, give our salute and say our words.'

Robert jumped up and gave the Wave salute. 'Mr Ross, we're all in the same team. Winners need discipline.'

'Now everybody together,' said Mr Ross.

◆

After school that afternoon David spoke to the other members of the football team. 'We must be more disciplined.' he said.

'What are you talking about?' one player asked.

'We lose games because we don't play together,' said David. 'We're not a team.'

'I don't want to lose any more games,' said another player.

'Yes, everybody in the school laughs at us,' said another.

'We can win,' said David. 'We're playing Clarkstown on Saturday. And we can win.'

'But what must we do?'

Eric looked at David. The Wave was something from their history lesson.

'Tell them,' said Eric. 'Tell them about the Wave.'

'All I know is that you start with some words,' said David. 'And this is the salute . . .'

Chapter 4 Members of the Wave

That evening Laurie told her mother and father about her history lesson.

Mrs Saunders looked at her daughter. 'I don't think I like it, Laurie.'

'But we're learning discipline, Mum. And how to work together. We're learning to be a team,' said Laurie.

'I want you to learn history,' said Mrs Saunders.

'You don't understand, Mum,' said Laurie. 'Mr Ross is showing

11

'You don't understand, Mum,' said Laurie. 'Mr Ross is showing us something important.'

us something important. And we're not forgetting about history. We're doing more homework now.'

'I think Laurie's history teacher knows what he's doing,' said Mr Saunders. 'I think it's good for the students to think about discipline.'

Mrs Saunders said, 'Too much discipline is dangerous.'

◆

Christy Ross also taught at Gordon High. That night Christy stayed late at the school. When she came home she found her husband with books all round him.

'How is your experiment going, Dr Frankenstein?' she asked.

'Very well,' said Ben. 'The students are much more interested in class. And they're doing their homework.'

Christy laughed. 'They can't be the same students I teach!'

'I'm very interested in this experiment,' said Ben. 'I want to see what will happen next.'

Christy was not happy. There was something about Ben's experiment she did not like. 'You must be very careful, Ben,' she said.

◆

David and Laurie walked to school together the next day.

'We need the Wave for our football team,' David said.

'I think you need better players,' Laurie said.

'We have good players,' said David, 'but we're not a good team. The Wave can help us. I talked to the team about it yesterday. Brian and Eric helped me.'

'My mother doesn't like it,' said Laurie.

'What does she know?' said David. 'Only the Wave members understand the Wave.'

◆

When the students arrived for their history lesson that day there was a big picture of a blue wave at the front of the room. Mr Ross stood next to the picture. The students went quickly to their places.

Mr Ross walked round the class and gave each student a yellow card. Each card had a picture of a wave on it. Under the picture of the wave were the words: MEMBER OF THE WAVE.

'What are these cards for?' asked Laurie.

The room was now very quiet. Ben turned round. 'Don't forget our rules, Laurie,' he said.

Laurie got up and stood by her desk. 'Mr Ross, what are these cards for?'

'They show that you are members of the Wave. Everybody in this room is now a member of the Wave. Now we can work together. Students, do you believe in the Wave?'

The students stood up by their desks. 'Mr Ross, yes!' they all said together.

'So now we're a team. You must always work together. You must never work against any other Wave member. Do you understand?'

'Mr Ross, yes!' said the class.

'Now you go and look for new members,' said Mr Ross, 'But every new member must understand our rules.'

Suddenly Robert stood up. 'Mr Ross,' he said. 'I think the Wave is great.'

Then Amy stood up. 'Mr Ross, Robert is right. I feel the same.'

David was pleased. He stood up. 'Mr Ross, we're now a team.'

Mr Ross was surprised. He wanted to stop talking about the Wave. He wanted to teach his usual lesson. But the students wanted more of the Wave.

'We'll give our salute,' he told the class. 'Then we'll say our words.'

'We're all in the same team. Winners need discipline,' said the students all together.

Ben Ross looked at his students in surprise. He saw that the Wave was not a game to them. They *were* the Wave now.

Mr Ross walked round the class and gave each student a yellow card.

Chapter 5   A Dangerous Experiment

At lunch that day all the Wave members sat at the same table. Brian, Brad, Amy, Laurie and David were there. Robert Billings walked in.

'Robert, come and sit with us,' said David. 'We're all members of the Wave.'

Robert gave the Wave salute and came to the table.

Suddenly Laurie said, 'I think this is all very strange.'

David turned to her. 'What's strange?' he asked.

'All the things we do for the Wave,' said Laurie.

'It's different,' Amy told her. 'That's why it feels strange.'

'Yes,' said Brad, 'we're all together now. That's what is great about the Wave. We're all members of the same team.'

'Do you think that everybody likes that?' Laurie asked.

'Who doesn't like it?' David asked.

Laurie felt her face go red. 'I don't think I like it,' she said.

Suddenly Brian pulled out his 'Member of the Wave' card. 'Don't forget that you are a Wave member, Laurie. You mustn't break Wave rules.'

'Laurie isn't breaking any rule,' said David.

'But she mustn't say bad things about the Wave,' said Robert quickly.

The others looked at Robert. Robert did not usually say anything. Laurie smiled.

'I'm happy that you're sitting with us, Robert,' she said. 'That's one good thing about the Wave. Now we're all in the same team.'

The students at Gordon High loved the Wave. Every day there were more new members. All round the school there were Wave pictures. Students gave the Wave salute when they met.

Ben Ross was very surprised. 'And my history students are working very well,' he told Christy. 'They want to say the Wave words and give the Wave salute in every lesson. But they do more homework than they did before.'

'I hear that the football team are all members now,' said Christy. 'But do you think that the Wave is good for the students? Are they learning anything?'

'Christy, the Wave is an experiment.' said Ben. 'There was no discipline in this school before I started it. Now I tell the students to do something and they do it. I think this new discipline is good for them.'

◆

Laurie sat on a desk in *The Grapevine* office. Other students sat on desks near her.

'It's always the same with this newspaper,' said Laurie. 'Everybody wants to see their names in *The Grapevine*. But nobody wants to do the work. Alex, where's your story about music?'

16

'Don't forget that you are a Wave member, Laurie. You mustn't break Wave rules.'

'What story?' said Alex. 'Oh yes, I remember. I'll do it next week.'

'Alex, you need discipline to write for a newspaper!' said Laurie. 'We must work as a team. I want your story tomorrow.'

Alex laughed. 'Are you a member of the Wave?' he asked.

'I'm in Mr Ross's class,' said Laurie. 'Everybody in our class is a member.'

'Everybody in the school is talking about the Wave,' said Alex. 'Write a story about it.'

Laurie looked at the others. 'Yes. Perhaps I will. It's a good story,' she said. 'We can ask the other students what they think.'

♦

Principal Owens wanted to see Ben Ross in his office. Was there something wrong? Ben knew that Principal Owens wanted to talk about the Wave.

On the way to Principal Owens' office Ben met many students. They all gave him the Wave salute.

The door was open, and Principal Owens sat behind his desk. Ben was surprised when the old man smiled at him. He looked down at Ben. 'Tell me what this Wave thing is about, Ben,' he said. 'Everybody in the school is talking about it.'

Ben told the story of his experiment.

'It's very strange, Ben,' said Principal Owens. 'Are the students learning anything?'

'They're doing better than before,' said Ben. 'I think the Wave is helping them.'

'I don't like these Wave salutes and Wave pictures,' said Principal Owens.

'It's all a game,' said Ben.

Principal Owens looked at Ben. Then he said, 'I'm not very happy about this thing, Ben. You must watch it very carefully. Remember that these are young people in your experiment. Sometimes we forget that they are young.'

'Everybody in the school is talking about the Wave,' said Alex.
'Write a story about it.'

Chapter 6   Anger and Fights

The next morning Laurie Saunders went to *The Grapevine* office. When she opened the door, she found a letter on the floor. The letter had her name on the front. Laurie closed the door and read the letter.

Dear Laurie

I am a student here at Gordon High. Three days ago my friends and I heard about this thing called the Wave. We went to Mr Ross's lesson to see what it was. Mr Ross told us about the Wave rules and the Wave words. Some of my friends thought the Wave was great. But I did not want to be a member.

The letter had her name on the front. Laurie closed the door and read the letter.

When the class ended we started to leave. But a boy from Mr Ross's class stopped me. 'Do you want to be members of the Wave?' he asked.

'No, I don't want to be a member,' I said.

'But the Wave is great,' the boy said to me. 'Everybody wants to be a member! Do you want to lose all your friends?'

'I'm sorry,' I said again, 'but I don't want to be a member.'

The boy was very angry. 'Soon it will be too late,' he said.

Too late for what? That's what I want to know.

There was no name at the bottom of the letter.

Alex came into the office. Laurie showed him the letter. 'Look at this! Look what the Wave is doing to this school,' she said. 'This student is afraid of the Wave. He didn't want to write his name on the letter. We must do something.'

'There is a big Wave rally this afternoon,' said Alex. 'All the Wave members are going.'

Suddenly Laurie heard a noise. It came from outside the door. She ran out and saw that there was a fight between two boys. One of the fighters was Brian Amman!

A teacher ran and stopped the fight. 'I'm taking you two to Principal Owens,' he said.

Brian turned to the other students, and gave them the Wave salute. 'We're all in the same team. Winners need discipline!' he said.

'Did you see that?'

Laurie turned to find David next to her. 'Was that fight about the Wave?' she asked.

'No, it was more than that,' said David. 'The other boy is called Deutsch. We don't like him because he doesn't help the others in the team.'

'But why did Brian say the Wave words?'

'Because he believes in those words. We all do.' said David.

'What about the other boy?' asked Laurie. 'Is he in the Wave?'

Laurie ran out and saw that there was a fight between two boys.
One of the fighters was Brian Amman!

'No,' said David. 'Deutsch doesn't believe in the team or the Wave. He only believes in Deutsch.'

Laurie did not say anything. David looked at his watch. 'It's time for the Wave rally. Come on!'

Laurie looked away. 'I'm not going, David,' she said.

'What?' David was surprised and angry. 'Why not?'

'Because I don't want to.'

'Laurie, this is a very important rally,' David said. 'All the new members of the Wave are going to be there.'

'David, I don't like what's happening with the Wave. I don't like what it's doing to this school.'

Now David was very angry. 'The Wave is doing great things for Gordon High,' he said. 'Now everybody is on the same team. Perhaps that's why you don't like it. Before, you were the best student in the class. You always knew the answers. Now we all work for the team. And you don't like it!'

'David! That's not true and you know it!' said Laurie angrily. 'You're wrong about the Wave. And you're wrong about me!'

David turned and walked away. Laurie watched him and felt very sad. She loved David very much. Was this the end between them?

Chapter 7   At the Football Game

The next week Laurie did not have lunch with David or go out with him. She worked on *The Grapevine* all week. She was surprised that Amy did not come to the office. But Laurie knew that her friend believed in the Wave.

'Amy doesn't know what we know,' Laurie told Alex. 'We must tell her all the bad things about the Wave.'

On Saturday Laurie went to the football game between Gordon High and Clarkstown school. She looked for Amy. Laurie and Amy always sat together at football games.

'Stop!'

Laurie stopped and turned round. It was Brad.

'Hello, Laurie. I didn't see it was you,' he said. Then he did the Wave salute.

Laurie did not move.

'Come on, Laurie,' said Brad. 'Salute me.'

'Why?' asked Laurie.

'Because it's part of the Wave,' said Brad.

'Did everybody here give you the Wave salute?' asked Laurie.

'All the members did,' said Brad.

Laurie was very angry. 'I want to go in,' she said. 'But I don't want to give the Wave salute.'

Brad's face went red. 'Laurie, please do the salute now. Then you can go in.'

'No,' said Laurie. 'This is wrong! You know it's wrong.'

Brad looked round and said. 'OK, you win. You can go in without the salute. I don't think anybody is looking.'

But now Laurie did not want to go in. 'Why are you doing this, Brad?' Laurie asked. 'You know it's wrong. Are you afraid of the other Wave members?'

'I'm not afraid of anyone, Laurie,' he said. 'And I don't like what you're saying. A lot of people saw that you were not at the Wave rally yesterday.'

'And?'

'I don't want to say any more.' Brad said.

Brad turned and walked away. Laurie went home. She did not see Gordon High lose the game with Clarkstown.

Chapter 8   Laurie's Story

Laurie went to see Amy. She showed her the story about the Wave in the new *Grapevine*.

Amy began to read the story. When she finished she turned to Laurie. She was not happy. 'You can't say these things about the Wave, Laurie,' she said.

'They're true, Amy,' said Laurie.

'No, Laurie,' said Amy. 'I don't believe that. I think you don't like the Wave because of your fight with David.'

'That's not true!' said Laurie. 'The Wave is doing very bad things to this school. Read what it says in our story.'

'I believe in the Wave,' said Amy. 'I believe that we're all a team. I want us to work together. You don't like it because you think you're better than us.'

'But Amy —'

'I must go,' said Amy. 'My lesson starts soon.'

Laurie felt very sad and very angry. Amy was her best friend. But now Amy walked away from Laurie, too.

♦

Ben Ross read Laurie's story about the Wave in *The Grapevine*. He was very surprised.

When school finished Christy came to Ben's room. 'Are you OK, Ben?' she asked.

Ben looked up from *The Grapevine*. 'I don't like this,' he said. 'Something is going wrong. I never wanted the students to fight about the Wave.'

'I'm hearing bad things too, Ben' said Christy. 'Many of the other teachers don't like your experiment.'

Ben walked to the window and looked out. Some students saw him. They gave Wave salutes. Ben turned to Christy, 'Most of the students believe in the Wave,' he said.

Christy did not think that was a good thing. But she stayed quiet.

♦

David Collins read *The Grapevine* with his friends. His face was sad. 'I don't understand Laurie. Why does she write these things about the Wave?' he asked.

'I'm hearing bad things too, Ben,' said Christy. 'Many of the other teachers don't like your experiment.'

Robert stood next to David. He was very angry. 'They aren't true!' he said. 'Somebody must stop her writing about us.'

'It's not important,' David told him.

'Yes, it *is* important,' Robert said. 'People will believe what they read.'

'I tried to talk to her,' Amy said. 'But she doesn't want to listen to us.'

'We can't stop Laurie writing about us,' David said. 'But we can show everybody that she's wrong! We can show people all the good things about the Wave.'

'But people are going to see Principal Owens in his office, too,' said Brian. 'They want to stop the Wave. Can you believe that?'

'We must stop Laurie Saunders,' said Robert.

'Don't worry, Robert,' said Brian. 'David and I will go and see Laurie.'

'But I don't think –'

David felt Brian's hand on his arm. 'You're the best person to talk to her, David,' he said.

'Yes, but why does Robert say those things about Laurie? I don't like it!'

'Dave, Laurie is trying to stop the Wave,' said Brian. 'You must talk to her. She'll listen to you.'

David did not know what to do. The Wave was important to him. But so was Laurie. 'Do you think that she'll listen to me, Brian?'

'You're the only person she *will* listen to!' said Brian. 'We'll wait for her after school tonight. Then you can go and talk to her.'

Chapter 9   A Sad Day for David

Ben Ross left school early. Christy thought she knew why. When she arrived home Ben was in the kitchen. In his hand was another book about the Nazis.

27

'What happened to you today?' Christy asked.

'I didn't feel well,' said Ben.

'Ben, we must talk about this Wave thing,' said Christy. 'I don't like what's happening at the school. Some of the teachers are going to see Principal Owens about it.'

'I know, I know! They don't understand the Wave,' Ben answered.

'Do *you* understand it, Ben?' his wife asked. 'Do you know what you're doing? Because nobody in the school thinks you do.'

'I know that,' Ben answered. 'They think I want to be a little Hitler.'

'Perhaps they're right!' said Christy. 'This experiment is doing something to you. And I don't like it!'

Ben put his head in his hands. He knew his wife was right. There *was* something wrong. But he did not know what to do. 'I thought you believed in me,' he said.

'I do believe in you,' said Christy. 'But I don't believe in this experiment. You must end the Wave, Ben!'

Ben jumped up. 'No, I won't do that. I can't do that!' he told his wife. 'I'm their teacher. These students are learning the most important lesson in their lives.'

'I hope that Principal Owens thinks the same,' said Christy. 'He wants to see you tomorrow morning.'

♦

Laurie left *The Grapevine* office late that evening. The road outside the school was dark and very quiet. Laurie felt a little afraid. The Wave was strong in Gordon High, and a lot of the Wave members were angry with Laurie.

Suddenly Laurie heard somebody behind her. She felt very afraid now. She began to run.

'Laurie!'

Laurie turned her head and saw David behind her.

'Wait for me, Laurie,' said David. 'I want to talk to you. It's very

'This experiment is doing something to you. And I don't like it!'

'Get your hands off me, David! I don't like the Wave! And I don't like you!'

important.' Laurie stopped. 'Where are the others, David?' she asked. 'You Wave members always do everything together.'

David was angry. 'Laurie, you must stop writing bad things about the Wave.'

'The Wave is the bad thing, David,' said Laurie.

'It is not,' said David. 'Laurie, we want you to be with us.'

'No,' said Laurie. 'I told you, I don't want to be a member. This is not a game.'

She started to walk away, but David walked after her. 'The Wave is good for everybody,' he said. 'You must see that, Laurie! The Wave *can* work.'

'I don't want it to work.'

David was very angry now. He put his hand on Laurie's arm.

'I want you to stop writing about the Wave, Laurie!' he said.

'No, I *will* write about the Wave,' Laurie said. 'The school needs to know! And you can't stop me!'

'We *can* stop you! And we will!'

Laurie turned to leave. David put his hand on her arm.

'Get your hands off me, David! I don't like the Wave! And I don't like you!'

Laurie tried to push David away. But David was very angry and pushed Laurie over. Then he put his hand to his mouth.

'Oh no! Laurie, are you OK? Laurie, I'm sorry! Why did I do that? Laurie, I'm sorry!'

Chapter 10   The Wave Must End!

'Ben, the Wave must end!' said Christy. 'I know you think it's important for your students. But you must end it tomorrow.'

'How can you say that?' Ben asked.

'You're a good teacher, Ben,' said Christy. 'But this experiment is bad for Gordon High. I want you to go to Principal Owens tomorrow. I want you to tell him that you're going to end the Wave.'

'Christy,' Ben said, 'I know it must stop. But I don't see how.'

'You started the Wave, Ben,' said Christy. 'You're its leader. And you must stop it . . . What was that noise? Is that somebody at the door?'

'I think it is,' said Ben. 'I'll go and see.'

Ben went to the door. 'Who is it?' he asked before he opened it.

'It's David Collins and Laurie Saunders, Mr Ross.'

Ben was very surprised but he opened the door. 'What are you doing here?' he asked. 'It's late.'

'Mr Ross, we must talk to you,' David said. 'It's very important.'

'Come in and sit down,' Ben said.

The two students came in and sat down. 'Mr Ross, you must help us,' said David.

'What is it?' Ben asked. 'What's wrong?'

'It's the Wave,' said David.

'Mr Ross, we know this is important to you,' said Laurie. 'But bad things are happening. Students are afraid.'

'Tonight I pushed Laurie over,' said David. 'And it was because of the Wave.'

'Mr Ross, you must end the Wave,' said Laurie.

Laurie and David looked at their teacher. For nearly a minute Ben did not speak. Then he said, 'You're right. I will end the Wave.'

'What are you going to do, Mr Ross?' David asked.

'I can't tell you now,' said Ben. 'But you must believe in me. I want you to say nothing to the other students. Can you do that?'

'Yes, Mr Ross,' said David.

Laurie looked at Ben. 'I don't know, Mr Ross.'

'Laurie, it's very important that we do it carefully. You must believe in me. I started this thing and I will end it. OK?'

'Mr Ross, you must end the Wave,' said Laurie.

Chapter 11   The Last Rally

'I have something to tell you about the Wave,' Mr Ross told his history students the next day. 'At five o'clock today there will be a rally. It will be for Wave members only.'

David smiled and looked at Laurie.

'The Wave is not an experiment in your history lesson,' said Mr Ross. 'It's much more than that. All across the country there are now Wave members. The Wave is getting bigger and bigger.'

Laurie looked very afraid and David stopped smiling. He jumped out of his place. 'Mr Ross, Mr Ross!'

'Sit down, David!' said Mr Ross.

'But, Mr Ross, you said –'

'Sit down, David!'

David sat down in his place. 'Now listen carefully,' said Mr Ross. 'This afternoon we will see our leader on the television. He is going to start the Wave in every school in America!'

David and Laurie jumped to their feet. They ran to the front of the room.

'Don't listen to him!' said David.

'We must stop the Wave,' said Laurie.

The room was very quiet. 'Go back to your places,' said Mr Ross. 'I'll speak to you after the lesson.'

After the lesson Mr Ross spoke to David and Laurie. 'Don't worry,' he said. 'I know what I'm doing. You must believe in me.'

'We did believe in you,' said Laurie. 'And believed in the Wave. Now we don't know what to believe.'

◆

School finished at four o'clock. Laurie and David did not want to wait for the rally. They left together.

'I don't know why I believed in it,' said David. 'And I don't

Laurie and David did not want to wait for the rally.

understand why the others believe in it now. Perhaps we're wrong about the Wave.'

'No, David, we're right,' said Laurie.

'Then why do the others not see it?'

'I don't know,' said Laurie. 'They don't want to listen. Perhaps they're afraid.'

For a minute they did not speak. Then Laurie said, 'Do you remember that film about the Nazis, David? The Wave is dangerous! We can't walk away from this. That's what the people in Germany did. We must go back to school. We must go to that rally.'

◆

There were more than two hundred students in the room. At the front there were two televisions. Above the televisions there were the Wave pictures.

Mr Ross walked to the front. The Wave members all stood up and gave the Wave salute.

'We're all in the same team. Winners need discipline,' they all said together.

Mr Ross put his hand up. The students were quiet.

'In a minute our leader will speak,' said Mr Ross. 'Robert, turn on the televisions.'

'Mr Ross, yes.'

Robert turned on the two televisions. Two hundred Wave members waited to see their leader.

But nothing happened. The televisions showed no pictures.

David and Laurie came into the room. 'What's happening?' asked David quietly.

'I don't know,' said Laurie.

The Wave members waited and waited. Then one student jumped up. 'There *is* no leader!' he said.

Ben walked over to one of the televisions. 'Yes, you have a leader!' he said.

Suddenly there was the same picture on the two televisions. 'There is your leader!'

'But it's Adolf Hitler!' said one of the students. 'How can Hitler be the leader of the Wave?'

'That photo is from the film we saw in Mr Ross's history lesson. The film about the Nazis!' said Laurie.

The room was now very quiet. The Wave members did not understand. Was Hitler their leader? But Hitler was the worst man in history!

'Now listen carefully,' said Ben. 'There is no Wave outside this school. There is no great leader.' Ben pointed to the picture of Hitler. 'Men like Hitler lead things like the Wave. You all thought you were better than the other students. The Nazis thought they were better than the Jews.'

Ben stopped and looked down at the students. 'I'm sorry that I

Suddenly there was the same picture on the two televisions.
'There is your leader!'

'I think it's good that this happened, Mr Ross,' said Laurie. 'We all learned a lot.'

started this. I didn't want to be your "Hitler". But that's what happened and I'm very sorry. Perhaps we *all* learned something from the Wave.'

David and Laurie walked slowly out of the room with all the others. Nobody spoke. Amy looked up and saw Laurie. She began to cry. 'I'm sorry, Laurie,' she said.

Behind her, David saw Eric and Brian. The three footballers stood together without a word. David felt bad for his friends. 'We must try and forget the Wave,' he told them. 'But we must not forget what it did to us. Do you understand?'

Eric smiled. 'I knew that it didn't work when we lost to Clarkstown,' he said.

Chapter 12   After the Wave

David and Laurie went back to see Mr Ross. The room was now very quiet. 'I'm sorry I didn't believe you, Mr Ross,' David said.

'No, it was good that you didn't,' Ben told him.

'Mr Ross, what's going to happen now?' asked Laurie.

'I don't know, Laurie,' said Ben. 'Perhaps we'll have a class to talk about what happened today.'

'I think it's good that this happened, Mr Ross,' said Laurie. 'We all learned a lot.'

'That's nice of you,' said Ben. 'But I'm not going to teach the Wave again next year!'

David and Laurie smiled.

◆

Ben watched the last students leave. He turned and saw Robert next to the television. The boy looked up. He began to cry.

It is very sad for Robert, Ben thought. He put his hand on his arm. 'Let's go for something to eat, Robert,' said Ben. 'There are some things I want to talk about.'

ACTIVITIES

Chapters 1–4

Before you read

1 Look at the pictures on the front of the book and page 10.
   a Who is the man? Who are the other people? Where are they?
   b What do you know about Adolf Hitler and the Nazis? Tell another
   student.
2 Find these words in your dictionary. They are all words about *football*
   and *teams*.
   member/team
   football/rule
   leader/discipline
   a Now write three sentences to show the meaning of the words.
   b Do you know any other words about football and teams? Tell
   another student.
3 Find these words in your dictionary.
   believe   lead   need   wave
   Write four sentences to show the meaning of the words.
4 Find these words in your dictionary.
   card   experiment   history   salute   strange   surprised
   Now use the words to finish these sentences.
   a I liked . . . . . lessons at school because the teacher was good.
   b Nazis carried a . . . . . and gave a . . . . . when they saw Hitler.
   c Something . . . . . happened and everybody was very . . . . . .
   d They used animals in the . . . . . to try to help ill people.

After you read

5 Who said these words? Who to?
   a 'Were all the Nazis bad people?'
   b 'All he thinks about is football.'
   c 'Discipline starts with how you sit.'
   d 'How is your experiment going, Dr Frankenstein?'
   e 'Only the Wave members understand the Wave.'

40

6 'Too much discipline is dangerous.' Why does Mrs Saunders say this? Do you think she is right? Why/why not?

Chapters 5–8

Before you read

7 When you were younger, were you a member of a team? Was the team good or bad for you? Talk to another student.

8 Find these words in your dictionary.
principal rally
  a Is the *principal* of a school important?
  b Do you think *rallies* can sometimes be dangerous? How?

After you read

9 Who are these people? What do you know about them?
  a Principal Owens
  b Laurie
  c David
  d Ben
  e Christy

10 Work with another student. Have a conversation.
  Student A: You are a member of the Wave and you like it. Tell another student why.
  Student B: You don't like the Wave. You think it is dangerous and don't want to be a member. Tell Student A why.

Chapters 9–12

Before you read

11 Laurie and David are in love but they have different ideas about the Wave. What do you think is going to happen to them? Can they stay friends?

After you read

12 Answer these questions:
  a What do the other teachers think about the Wave?
  b 'Laurie, I'm sorry!' Why is David sorry?

41

c Who goes to see Mr Ross at his home? Why?

d Who do the students see on television at the rally?

e Is Mr Ross going to teach the Wave next year?

13 Mr Ross says, 'We all learned something from the Wave.' What did you learn?

Writing

14 Write a letter from Laurie to a friend. Tell the friend about the Wave and your problems with David.

15 Write a newspaper story about the Wave for *The Grapevine*. You can write about these things. When did the Wave start? What do the Wave members do? What are the Wave rules? Why is the Wave good or bad?

16 Who did you like most in the story? Write everything you know about the person and why you like him/her most.

17 When you were younger, did anything strange happen to you at school? Write about it.